REVIEWS OF SOULS IN LOVE

Souls in Love has an ambitious aim, to support lovers in deepening and sustaining the loving essence of their relationship by exploring contextual intimacy through poems. The weave of feminine and masculine poetic expression contained within this volume opens many delicious possibilities for healing dialogue between lovers. In the revelation of one couple's honest relating, we find the universal truths of love. You will recognize both your light and shadow-self dancing on these pages. May it open the doors of your heart ever wider.

Davina Mackail
Hay House author and Medicine woman

Sam Yau and Sophie Rouméas' *Souls in Love* has truly cracked the code to the ineffable, mystical quality of Romantic Love. A force so powerful, so all-encompassing, so incomprehensible, it cannot be defined by words of description or analysis like science or philosophy. Only the words of the poet can traverse the chasm between the mystical and the sacred.

As a couple, as a man and a woman, as two souls wandering this world in search of the true meaning of Life, their sacrifice in the caldron of romantic love and relationship has birthed a profound gift presented to the world of souls wandering an austere world where true love seems to most, illusive.

These words, smithed into tapestries of shimmering light, offer up a healing balm that soothes a weary soul that is thirsting for this one quality of life. Here is offered not just a taste, but a feast.

James Hyman
Deep Emotional Release Therapist

Souls In Love touched my soul in so many ways that I never expected a book could. The words flowed off the pages into my heart and my body activating so many emotions and feelings within me. As I read the Poems by Sam and Sophie, I could feel and connect to the deep intimacy held in each page and every word. Not only the love I felt displayed for each other through the essence of each poem. But I felt their love and intimacy for life itself. Within the pages of *Souls in Love*, I witnessed beautiful and sometimes raw descriptions of life & love, a look at their soul's intimate journey. This powerful book taught me that love is multifaceted, vulnerable, powerful, beautiful, joyful, and painful. Love is experienced with many different people in our lives in many ways. *Souls in Love* does not discriminate against love in any way. Instead, it embraces all facets unconditionally. Sam and Sophie, I didn't think a book like this could be written, that captured the multidimensions of love. But here you are, displaying love in its most vulnerable, healing, and loving way.

Renée Vidal
The Soul's Journeys Podcast
Quantum Healing Hypnosis Technique Therapist

Souls in Love put me in a deep state of awe. Awe for Sam and Sophie and their surrender to love. Awe for the ease and gorgeous craft with which each writes so intimately about the experience of love. And awe for the sheer audacity of this experiment - 2 poets writing about love as they travel the love terrain together.

A mature reader that I am, I cherish the lived wisdom of these poems. These are poems of the simple moment, of love being everywhere, all around us. They are also poems of two people with complex pasts that infuse their experience of love. And I read these poems as poems of hope - hope for the continued possibility of opening the gates of our gardens to another, body and soul. I envision reading *Souls in Love* again and again - it is that good.

Achim Nowak
Author/Podcaster/Executive Coach

Historically, love poems have been written by one only lover. It is a rare opportunity to find two poets in love writing jointly. Fluid, like water, their words bring us through their voyage from one soul to another. First, discovering a common dream they did not know they had, then accepting change, and finally embracing a new reality. Understanding is not the job of feelings; knowledge is. We know that if we touch the soul of the other, our life will forever change. But if we do not, we will not be able to continue breathing. So, we crawl out of ourselves and dare beyond memories, fears, ghosts, and misery. Beyond the pain that we hid in the bottom drawer of our existence so long ago. And we find peace reflected in the eyes of each other... They say that love happens when we dream it. The poets show us that love happens when the dream finally has a face.

Maria D. Bermudez
Professor of Sociology

Souls In Love is a new book of forty-two poems by two extra-ordinary talented poets, Sophie Rouméas and Sam Yau. Both poets complement each other's verses with deep insights into the multi-facet meaning of true, blissful love, which emanates from the beauty within the universal souls of all living life forms. As all true artists do, the exquisite poems will capture the reader's attention and take them on a metaphysical/physical journey in the majestic realms of love.

Michael Levy
Author poet philosopher
www.pointoflife.com

Souls in Love is a remarkable and transformative book on the nature of sacred sexuality and the true power of non-attached cosmic soul love. The deeper conscious truths and the way that Sam and Sophie combined their connection with universal love and the heart of embodiment through their poetry are truly powerful and spark a remembrance of truth within the soul of the reader. This book takes over the taboo of sex and spirituality and guides you into the recognition of what it truly is, the absolute most powerful creative life force energy available to all of us. The energy that gives life, love, and a connection to the true essence of your innermost being. Deep wisdom and power. Thank you, Sam and Sophie, for bringing forward deep gnosis to humanity.

Kara Goss
Author, Speaker, Mentor

Souls in Love is a masterpiece that we all wish we had written. There are so many beautiful gems of wisdom, so many profound universal insights that they defy any attempt to summarize them. Sam and Sophie are poets supreme, and beloveds who are compassionately moved to share with us their unfolding life together. The inevitable challenges of two humans in a relationship are also addressed, which adds to the authentic context of this soul-to-soul dialogue. Most importantly for me, this powerful weaving of poetry gives much-needed insight into the centrality of Love in the soul's lifelong journey to the divine.

J. Phillip Jones
Author, **Transcendence: Finding Peace at the End of Life**
Associate Publisher, Mandala Publishing

If you are in a relationship or long for a harmonious and passionate commitment, then this book is for you. Sam Yau and Sophie Rouméas have powerfully woven a captivating love journey that resonates with the human spirit. Their poetic story emphasizes unconditional love for self and others, explores the balance between independence and interdependence, validates the depth of connection through sensuality and physical intimacy, and eloquently ignites the fire within the heart and soul. Their poems provoke reason to pause and reflect and vibrantly inspire. The accompanying artwork is breathtaking. *Souls in Love* is quite simply, an exquisite and transcendent masterpiece!

Dr. Kimberly Schehrer
Teen Breakthrough Expert
www.afi4me.com

Imagine peering through a garden wall and observing two flowers choosing their blossoms, their beauty, their brilliance. That was my experience as I read *Souls in Love* by Sam Yau and Sophie Rouméas—a silent witness to a journey of love over international borders and personal boundaries. From the beginning, *Souls in Love* moves the reader through the cultivation of Sam and Sophie's relationship and the personal evolution of each. *Souls in Love* is sensual and sexy. It is mind-provoking and soul-searching. "In pleasing me / you lose part of you / In loving / you become expansive." A beautiful read.

Kay Clark-Uhles
Writer, Editor, Author of **Parts, Pieces & Particulars:**
A Primer for Single Moms Raising Sons & Single Dads Raising Daughters
mindwise.soulworks@gmail.com

Webs of prismatic emotions fuel individual experiences
And still each individual relates to the depictions laid out bare.
Such an experiential conglomeration of artworks and poems
Makes understanding the world we live in have a little more air.

Naveli Garg
Psychology student at UC Davis
www.NaviNiti.com

This collection of poems is embedded with romantic notes of intimacy fluidly laced together, inviting and encouraging the reader to linger on every word. Painting pictures of lovers entwined on a soul level, the poetry awakens the reader to desire and connection. *Souls in Love* is a dessert for the eyes and delicately, rhythmically, and powerfully reminds the reader that love is an adventure worth savoring.

MacKenzie Nelson
#1 International Best Selling-Author/ Podcast Host
www.mackenziekaynelson.com

Two souls becoming one, to be contained within each other and yet grow into their own, is the magic of love. *Souls in Love* recognizes the divine within themselves and the divine within each other while continuously learning to honor the union. Sophie Rouméas and Sam Yau have captured the essence of this eternal love that transcends materiality to build that deep and lasting connection. This collection of poetry will move you and guide your own soul in ways you are yet to imagine!

Dr. Kasthuri Henry
Ph.D. CEO of Kas Henry Inc & Founder of Ennobled for Success Institute

Souls in Love is a collection of poems celebrating newfound love and joy. Standing vulnerable in their poetry, these lovers bare their heart and soul in the celebration of their union together.

Maureen Ryan Blake
Maureen Ryan Blake Media Productions

Sam and Sophie have courageously shared these most secret and treasured moments - merging their own personal life stories, inspirations, sorrows, and hurts, and combined talents into one harmonious and powerful voice. An honest voice. One we are grateful to hear.

While reading this immensely beautiful poetry, I heard two melodies simultaneously - one deep, confident masculine and another high, multi-dimensional feminine - harmonizing themselves into one magnificent symphony of Love. Immersed in reading, countless love stories were running through my mind. It started first in the Garden of Eden, continued through the generations, reaching the streets of Paris, then migrating to the east coast of the United States - touching the entire world with a great "Love Story." Films, music, books, paintings, and poetry. Love is undeniably the most vital phenomenon in this world, it is so profoundly important to us, and yet we are often turning away. We become scared of Love, shy away, and feel unworthy, yet inevitably continue searching.

I caught myself thinking, "Such a blazing power beaming through every poem. Why does this experience reading Sam and Sophie's poetry feel almost supernatural?" It opened a treasure chest, of melodies, movies, and countless love stories. It's us. It's humanity. It's our history. It's our ancestors. Our DNA. Our memory. And Love was, is, and will forever be the most important and most powerful substance on this planet and beyond. I believe it is what God is made of.

Finally, I got my answer. The only way to really experience the supernatural is to walk in Love, to be present in Love, not to shy away, but be right at the epicenter of it. And this book, I believe, is right there, as it should be by divine destiny.

With gratitude, dear Sam and Sophie, for your honesty, passion, and your Love for each other and all of us, who will be privileged to read this magnificent Art in Poetry.

Olena Zavakevych
Artist, Painter

Souls in Love
Sam Yau and Sophie Rouméas
Clear Source Books

Published by Clear Source Books, Laguna Beach, CA
Copyright ©2022 Sam Yau (Ching Yuen) and Sophie Rouméas
All rights reserved.

No part of this publication may be reproduced, stored in a retrieval system, or transmitted in any form or by any means, electronic, mechanical, photocopying, recording, scanning, or otherwise, except as permitted under Section 107 or 108 of the 1976 United States Copyright Act, without the prior written permission of the Publisher. Requests to the Publisher for permission should be addressed to Permissions Department, Clear Source Books Sam@SamYauPoetry.com.

Project Management and Book Design: Davis Creative, LLC | CreativePublishingPartners.com
Publicity: Rebecca Hall Gruyter/RHG Media Productions | YourPurposeDrivenPractice.com
Poetry Coach: Rachel Kann
Proofreader: Kay Clark-Uhles

Publisher's Cataloging-in-Publication
(Provided by Cassidy Cataloguing Services, Inc.).

Names: Yau, Sam, author. | Rouméas, Sophie, author.
Title: Souls in love / Sam Yau and Sophie Rouméas.
Description: Laguna Beach, CA : Clear Source Books, [2022]
Identifiers: ISBN: 978-1-7363700-3-2 (hardback) | 978-1-7363700-4-9 (paperback) | 978-1-7363700-5-6 (ebook) | LCCN: 2022921159
Subjects: LCSH: Interpersonal relations--Poetry. | Sensuality--Poetry. | Intimacy (Psychology)--Poetry. | Soul mates--Poetry. | Individual differences--Poetry. | LCGFT: Love poetry. | BISAC: POETRY / General. | FAMILY & RELATIONSHIPS / Love & Romance.
Classification: LCC: PS3625.A8 S68 2022 | DDC: 811/.6--dc23

ATTENTION CORPORATIONS, UNIVERSITIES, COLLEGES AND PROFESSIONAL ORGANIZATIONS:
Quantity discounts are available on bulk purchases of this book for educational, gift purposes, or as premiums for increasing magazine subscriptions or renewals. Special books or book excerpts can also be created to fit specific needs. For information, please contact Sam Yau, Sam@SamYauPoetry.com (USA) or Sophie Rouméas sophie.Rouméas@gmail.com (Europe).

GRATITUDE

Each poem of *Souls in Love* is illustrated by an artwork dear to us: we feel grateful to every artist who created the paintings, sculptures, and photographies included in our book. You will find their name and the title of their artwork in the Artwork Credits section.

A special thanks to the contemporary artists who accepted to be part of our book *Souls in Love*.

Olena Zavakevych, with her sublime painting inspired by the poem *I Can't Wait to Meet you*, from Sam Yau's first book, *Soul's Journey*, 2020.

Giorgio Dante, with his divine painting *Poi Tornò All' Eterna Fonte*, from his exhibition *Les Ténèbres et la Lumière*, in Le Palais des Papes of Avignon, France, 2021.

Gratitude for Rachel Kann, outstanding writer, poet, and coach, who helped me, Sophie, polish my poems! Her sincere and committed listening allowed my expression to be closer to the subtleties of the English and American languages while preserving the essence of my initial French writing.

To the artists, our friends, and our relatives who directly and indirectly supported us and encouraged our journey along this book creation, and to the visible and invisible inspiration, the creativity and love itself, thank you.

TABLE OF CONTENTS

Preface 1

SOULS IN LOVE — 5

Souls in Love – *by Sam Yau* 7
The Hummingbird – *by Sophie Rouméas* 11
I Can't Wait to Meet You – *by Sam Yau* 13
Souls' Encounter – *by Sophie Rouméas* 15

KINDRED SPIRITS — 19

Infused – *by Sam Yau* 21
Wine Tasting – *by Sam Yau* 23
How Do We Know – *by Sophie Rouméas* 25
Love and Shadow – *by Sam Yau* 27

LOVE ALCHEMY — 29

I Transcendence

Transcendence – *by Sophie Rouméas* 31
Re-creating – *by Sam Yau* 35
The Gem-Seed of Intention – *by Sophie Rouméas* 37
Full Union in Love – *by Sam Yau* 39
Lisbon – *by Sophie Rouméas* 41

II Passion

Yours, Spontaneously – *by Sam Yau* 45
Will I Dare You? – *by Sophie Rouméas* 47
Sensing – *by Sam Yau* 51
The Red Snow – *by Sophie Rouméas* 53
In This Silence – *by Sam Yau* 55

LOVE GARDEN — 57

A New Garden – *by Sophie Rouméas* 59
Your Inner Garden – *by Sam Yau* 63
Invitation to Your Senses – *by Sophie Rouméas* 67
Love in a Cage – *by Sophie Rouméas* 71

LOVE AND GROWTH   **73**

    Interdependence – *by Sam Yau* 75
    Hold the Space – *by Sophie Rouméas* 77
    Reciprocity – *by Sam Yau*. 79
    Letter to My Sons – *by Sophie Rouméas*. 81
    Love and Religion – *by Sophie Rouméas* 87
    💜 – *by Sophie Rouméas*. 89

LOVE AND HEALING   **91**

    Return to Love – *by Sam Yau* 93
    Return to Wholeness – *by Sam Yau*. 95
    Residual Matter – *by Sophie Rouméas*. 97
    The Misunderstanding – *by Sam Yau* 101
    Womanity's Shadow – *by Sophie Rouméas* 103
    Acceptance – *by Sam Yau*. 105

LOVE AND ART   **107**

    An Incessant Dialogue – *by Sophie Rouméas* 109
    Vincent – *by Sam Yau*. 113

LOVE AND CONSCIOUSNESS   **115**

    Traveling in Reality – *by Sophie Rouméas*. 117
    The Path – *by Sam Yau* 121
    Conscious Silence – *by Sophie Rouméas* 123
    Step into the Stream – *by Sam Yau* 125
    Archetypes – *by Sophie Rouméas* 127
    The Nature of Love – *by Sam Yau* 129

About the Poets. 131
Artwork Credits 133

PREFACE
by Sam Yau

Souls in Love originated from a conversation Sophie and I had on a three-hour train ride from Annecy to Paris in October 2021.

In this conversation, we explored many questions. What is the essence of romantic love? How can a couple ensure the flame of passion endure? What are the secrets to balancing independence and interdependence? How can lovers grow together instead of apart? Why is the union at all levels of our being—soul, mind, emotions, and body—necessary for the most profound intimacy? What is the role of our souls in romantic relationships?

These inquiries provide a contextual backdrop for conceiving and writing the poems in this collection.

Why we fall in love with another person and how we sustain the glow of love and passion cannot be understood just by rational analysis. To the extent love remains a mystery, poetry is an ideal vehicle for its expressions, which are plentiful in *Souls in Love*.

But we have a more extended aim, which is to reveal through our verses a framework for navigating love relationships. While not commonly done, we nevertheless deployed poetry as the literary genre for deliberating on this ecstatic and complex intersubjective human experience.

Souls in Love was written from our souls' perspectives. The soul is the part of each of us that connects to the source. As our true self, the soul embarks on a human journey to experience embodied love. Every revelation of love, including physical intimacy, is a soul-in-action.

Souls in Love illuminates intimacy as the essence and purpose of romantic love. Fueled by passion and rooted in shared commitment and values, a deep soul connection cascades into a joyful union at all levels—soul, mind, heart, and body—and awakens to a longing to live a loving and sensual life. Our poems explore the alchemy between two lovers that keeps the flame blazing.

Souls in Love is dedicated to lovers seeking blissful intimacy and lasting love in a committed relationship.

PREFACE
by Sophie Rouméas

From the same planet, yet Sam and I come from two different cultures, each imbued with our respective lives: Man and woman each previously married, each parent of loving children, and as many variances in our professional missions, ages, and countries of origin; nevertheless, fate has made our paths converge.

A love story requires different qualities of being that allow everyone to flourish in the space-time of the relationship. Far from the clichés that everything is easy and magical in love, an encounter between two souls recognizes the virtue of intention and communication. Self-awareness, a clear knowledge of one's own values, desires, and needs are all appreciated requirements for a genuine story. Magic can thus be born, from which the soul will act naturally and reciprocate with grace and commitment.

Love has this marvelous property of connecting to other dimensions of oneself and the Other, but also of the contemporary world, the universe, the sacredness, and art too.

Souls in Love is about consciousness, intimacy, growth in love. The love that awakens, opens wider the windows of the soul and the heart; the love that balances action and contemplation; the love that heals and transcends differences, the love that creates.

The 42 poems express facets of the multi-dimensionality of love. From this non-exhaustive and subjective topic, Sam and I share our expression with the reader by drawing on our personal experiences and the reflections manifested along our respective and synchronous life journey.

We designed the book in eight sections: the souls in love, from kindred spirit to opening up to the alchemy of love, then the cultivation of the lovers' inner garden, the personal growth within love, the healing invitation, and ultimately, love meeting art and consciousness.

We wrote our poems during our travels over a year. The south of France and its varied lights; Paris, the city of lovers; Lisbon and its many colors; Seville and its mystical soul; California and its dynamic nature—have been some of our extraordinary frames for writing.

Aware that our story makes us revisit some universal aspects of what the essence and substance of love is, our ambition is to invite the reader to take a poetic break and find a breeding ground for reflection, inspiration, and reverie.

Souls in Love

The Hummingbird

I Can't Wait to Meet You

Souls' Encounter

SOULS IN *Love*

By Sam Yau

The day I met you
I was so taken by your eyes
they were all I could see

Two brilliant rays of light
reaching deep into my soul

At the end of that fateful day
I was still dazed by the encounter

That night in my dream
I stood alone on a beach
under a silvery full moon
against a starless night sky

I gazed over the horizon

The ocean's faraway waves
surged taller and taller
roaring toward me

I had no fear

The sparkling
thundering
waves washed over me

Souls in Love

I was overwhelmed
by a divine universal love for you

I knew only your name
I remembered only your eyes
I searched the Internet for your name
confirmed it was you by your eyes

That was the beginning
of my heart's journey
in unconditional love

A love that I know is true
without a shred of doubt

A love that just is
no need to know why

A love that is as boundless
and pure as how I feel
when I look into a vast
cloudless translucent blue sky

Sam Yau

A love that demands
nothing from you
rejects nothing in you

A love in which one soul
retastes the eternal bond
with another soul

A love that is more
healing in giving
than receiving

A love that flows
through the divine spark
in our souls
from beyond

THE Hummingbird

By Sophie Rouméas

From the sacred mountains
in the old New World,
Medicine revealed to me
a memory to remember.

There is, for all beings,
a place in someone's heart,
a place on earth to land.

This place is revealed when the soul
is ready to receive
the energy of perfection—
a place where the self has only harmony
to evolve and resource in.

There is a being waiting for you,
somewhere,
and they keep calling you.

Hear the vibrations of the world—
they guide your actions
towards your destiny.
Don't think about time anymore,
nor space.

For a moment, leave
all benchmarks and ambition.
The Cosmic Clock
will reveal itself
in the letting go.

There is a being waiting for you,
somewhere,
and they keep calling you.

It is said, "You will leave your father and mother."
Will you walk your own path?
Time dissolves, the noise subsides.
In the silence, you finally hear
the voice of the way.

May you meet the hummingbird,
appreciate her philosophy.
She flies gracefully
between the winds.

She knows everything, every perfume,
all space and all time.
She shines with no limit—
this is the essence of her mission.
She is there to show you:

There is a being waiting for you,
somewhere,
and they keep calling you.

Once you meet,
the medicine of your union
will emerge in due time.
Thus, the legend of love on Earth
can perpetuate and welcome
more souls in search of bliss and home.

I CAN'T WAIT TO MEET *You*

By Sam Yau

When I see your face for the first time
you lift your gaze to meet mine

Time freezes
everyone else fades away
we know our destiny

Fired-up neurons trance-dance in unison
we dive into each other with no fear

We soar to heaven, sink to hell
unleash our best and our worst
mirror each other's light and shadow
we grind at each other's humanness
in joy, in pain, we grow together

No matter how many times
we separate and reunite
we always find our way back
to one another

We recognize our original faces
remember our eternal bond
intertwined for many lifetimes
forever in each other's embrace

To see and be seen
in our soul-essence
is to be in God's presence

SOULS' *Encounter*

By Sophie Rouméas

Naked before you,
my soul comes forward without fear.
I know my past torments,
my strengths, my weaknesses,
my light and my mission.

I anticipate your questions,
even the ones you won't ask.
I don't know everything about you,
but I know enough to recognize you.

I first met you in dreams and
meditations. And today,
in this past-life workshop.

In this reality,
it is not your face
that is familiar to me first,
it is the essence of your soul.

Our energies recognize
and greet each other
before our bodies do.

Then your voice—its vibration—
initiates an ascent of my frequency.

At this moment,
we are soul to soul,
like two old friends.

It will take us four years
to choose intimacy.

There are moments
in our existence
when we encounter synchronicity.
It manifests its presence
to remind us of our divinity.
It gives us signs along the way,
we can choose to perceive them.

The meeting of two souls
is not free from turmoil:

See the ocean and its riptides,
successions of swells,
changes in direction,
crosswinds.

What characterizes a souls' encounter
is a space free of judgment.
In you, I reveal myself,
in me, you are reborn to yourself.

Life is a sharing.

I become the vase of your ideas
you blossom in my inner waters.

Souls' Encounter

We bring to each other the light
of our past shadows,
primordial matter
that both our souls love to transmute
in a furrow of wisdom.

There is a conceiving force
emphasizing discernment
and unconditional appreciation
of what simply is.

It is said that a spiritual life
is stripped of all uselessness.

With you, my soul-flame,
every flower, every star
every object and
every morning,
becomes a raison d'être.

Living in grace does not prevent
us from embodying
our human experience.
It is a conscious choice
to walk through life
like a garden.

From morning to night,
we scatter our seeds of intention.

The kitchen
becomes a laboratory
wherein we infuse universal tenderness.

The living room,
a place of intellectual emanation,
a dialogue between hearts and minds.

The bathroom,
a spa ritual of purification
for all our senses to be accurate
in transmission and reception.

Our bedroom at night,
a sacred space
for our carnal dimension
and rest.

We are happy to support each other,
independent and together in our evolution.
Then, we enjoy sharing the happiness
with other friendly souls,
from here and beyond.

The outside thus becomes an opportunity
to breathe synchronicity
and to manifest it too,
because when we amplify
this soul energy,

the world around us becomes
an uplifting world.

KINDRED
Spirits

Infused

Wine Tasting

How Do We Know

Love and Shadow

Infused

By Sam Yau

A circle of aspen trees
outstretch their branches for us
to lie beneath their canopy
the leaves rustle in the gentle breeze
shimmer in the morning sun

Above the foliage, clouds swirl-waltz
against the satiny blue sky, celebrating
the melding of two kindred spirits

Song thrushes fly-dance above us, chirping
There is a place for us, us alone

You lay your hand on mine
while we lie on the green grass
a fireball stoked by our hearts
twirls between our palms
we are floating up, up and away

The fire you ignited in my soul
is burning bright
spreading out of control

I am infused with you.
I am drunk in our co-vibrations

Your hand has never left
maybe it never will

WINE *Tasting*

By Sam Yau

I've been the person
who'd fall for
the first one
who came along

This time
I'd change

I would

look
swirl
sniff
sip
and savor

the exquisitely curated
rich varietals
in the perfect
sequence

But I can no longer
delude myself

can't hide behind
an idyllic new life
you're not the
 center of

my fear of
being trapped
in a single taste

This morning
I woke up engulfed
in the pain of the
looming separation

How I would
pine for you
when the iron bird
fades into the cloud

How I would
run away
in clever ways
only to find
your face swirling
in my heart

Once more
I tore the
tasting menu
to pieces

There is only one

HOW DO WE *Know?*

By Sophie Rouméas

The physicality of being,
emotions of the heart,
vibrations of the soul…

The gateways to love
are varied and diverse.
With so many paths,
how do we know we love?

Like an eel in the hands,
words spin and slip away,
how do we know we love?

I call upon my curiosity,
the final station of my sobriety.

To love is to be drunk,
not on wine, but emotions—
and to surrender to them.

To love is to be wise,
to embrace the blessings,
welcome the sorrows too.

Love is this dichotomy,
this constant movement
between what I initiate
and what we generate.

Love calls for boldness,
tenderness and surrender—
a hint of attitude.
Above all, to love is to be.

From the present to all other times,
it is to reinvent,
dare to dream, feel and share.

It is being with you
what I would not be without you.
It is to live this uniqueness
of what life invites us
to manifest and create
by bringing us together.

Love and Shadow

By Sam Yau

The day I met you, I burst through my heart
and rocketed to the edge of the universe and back

I know of no love so boundless, so freeing
it demands nothing of you; it rejects nothing in you

Day after day, your soul's blinding light shines through
facet by facet, your iridescent radiance grows until

you become the sun, the moon, and all the stars in the sky
you catapult me right into the center of my divinity

I stand naked in front of you, immersed in your luminosity, unaware
that the shadow flicker-dances with the shimmering like friends

The foreboding of the inevitable breakup looms. The distant heartache
beat by beat, leaches out the bubbling joy from the now

When you show me your blazing love poem to your previous lover
a vinegar-fed fire snakes its scorching green flame from my stomach to my heart

Light and shadow, love and jealousy, are not strange bedfellows
it is me who is inflicted. Your pristineness remains unblemished

I wish I could be in the moment, lost in the bliss of my love for you
I wish I could scatter the future, or my fear of it, in the capricious wind

Love ALCHEMY

I TRANSCENDENCE

Transcendence

Re-creating

The Gem-Seed of Intention

Full Union in Love

Lisbon

Transcendence

By Sophie Rouméas

I want to travel life like poetry.
Life answers, *Let's travel each other.*

I travel from word to word
as we travel from age to age.

I've met Verlaine, Rimbaud, and even Marcel.
I've plucked Baudelaire's flowers,
smelled the rose of *The Little Prince*,
filled my senses with
the dampness of morning.

I've walked fields of poppies
where the sun bathed me in its light—
oceans and deserts, too,

I left the Garden of Eden
to explore the dimensions of humanity.

I've met happy people, controlling men,
powerful women, helpless children.

I've lived in countries
where the flag of innocence
does not exist.

I've seen sometimes
that love was a transaction.

I've crossed rivers to find love.
It burned my skin,
my heart.

I drew on the sweetness of my womb,
breathed in the Passion of Man,
then asked Christ to save me.

I touched the shadows of my soul,
turned my gaze from them,
met the depths of my being,
wished with all my might
for the day to come back.

I turned over the stones of the garden,
looked for answers
to questions that didn't have any,
found more questions not supposed to be asked.
A subject becomes what we make of it.

I traveled outside of my body,
outside of my own footsteps
even lost my personality.

I finally found my original essence
at the bottom of myself.

Transcendence

I've smiled at smiles,
cried in response to tears,
sang along with intoxicating music,
embraced my life mission,
reassured and guided disillusioned souls.

We voyaged *In Search of Lost Time*—
the alchemical recipe of the Philosopher's Stone—
the entry into absolute consciousness.

Transcendence is the engaged presence
to a flower, a tree, a bird, a mist,
the love of two bodies, the caress of a kiss,
the taste of a ripe fruit, the scent of a sunrise,
the movement of a wave, the silence of the mind.

Transcendence also appears when a child is born of love,
(though adults sometimes leave
the transcended state
while the ego seeks maturity.)
*Dear children, the clock is ticking,
the forests evolve from season to season.*

Above all, transcendence
is the dance of the flame of life,
no matter what awakens the inner vibration.

This morning, I dreamt of you:
You walked towards me,
took my hand, and introduced me
to the tree that contains your dreams.

I am moved.
It is an honor, a gift
to be offered entrance
to someone's garden.
I keep my hand in yours,
fill myself
with your presence.

This morning, I will leave
everything not necessary.
I will savor the air around me,
infused with your dream company.

I enter a new transcendence.
I have found my meant-to-be,
the one who walks the words.

This morning, I will stop walking
and sit in silence at the foot of your tree.

I watch you sleep.
When you open your eyes,
I will kiss you.

Re-creating

By Sam Yau

I can't distinguish
our lovemaking from
our poetrymaking

In the twirling wind
fly our tender words
and passionate kisses

We become poetry
to each other

This primal wildfire

This burning desire
now seared upon
our body and soul

When the dust settles
our new love poem
emerges from the ashes

In your iris
I see my reflection
I am no longer the same

From each flare
we re-create each other
a new image
sculpted by words

THE GEM SEED OF *Intention*

By Sophie Rouméas

During our first encounter,
your story beat in my heart.
My whole being mourned your past tears,
and my soul called for your peace.

Your father-pain resonated
in my mother-depth—
and my daughter- and sister-depth.

For months: not one
exchange as kindred spirits
without the desire to comfort you.

One day, I found a key.
I didn't know what to do with it,
until the rhythms of destiny
pulsed again in my veins.

My heart opened to love,
roused the wind of passion.
My body, in a twirl, my
self, alchemizing,
from you, I dared
to receive the gem seed of Intention.

What a surprise,
to feel in my center
the beat of desire;
melodies to compose.

I embrace every note from you:
the salt of your skin
the cinnabar of your being,
my yin harmonizes with you,
your yang transmutes with mine.

I love these moments of delight
that we create in Paris,
this rediscovered music
amplified in the lights of the city.

Montmartre is our garden
of blooming poetry.
We visit Oscar Wilde
in Saint-Germain, toast De Beauvoir
and Hemingway aux Deux Magots,
sing Serge Gainsbourg on the rue de Verneuil,
walk the trees of the Tuileries,
smile back at Mona Lisa,
pick her rose at last.

At nightfall,
we return to the cosmos.

FULL UNION IN *Love*

By Sam Yau

My love, hear my whisper

Like hummingbirds
we flutter our wings
a thousand times
hover in mid-air
tasting our nectar

We know what sweetness is

My love, hear my whisper

Like moths
fearless of the flame
we open all our senses
surrender our bodies
sating our sacred desire

We know what pleasure is

My love, hear my whisper

Like butterflies
we redissolve ourselves
merging in one cocoon
morphing in bliss
into our new destiny

We know what happiness is

My love, hear my whisper

Like eagles
we soar into the clouds
you and I become one
hurling ourselves into
the center of our divinity

We know what ecstasy is

My love, hear my whisper

You lift me up to heights
far beyond where I could
ever dare to imagine

This numinous intimacy of full union

My love, hear my whisper

I am in deep gratitude to you

Lisbon

By Sophie Rouméas

Marcos: the poet
in the parvis.
He distributes odes
to the population.
He is from Germany.
Heroic choice
to be a poet of the streets.
The cathedral, Our Lady of the Martyrs,
surrounds him with her fervor.

Marjoleine: the entrepreneur
on the go,
she is about to open her restaurant
in Holland.
She is traveling with her mother,
savoring the spicy delights,
Time Out Market,
before the non-stop
of her new life.
This city rocks her.

All these people from here and elsewhere,
breathing the multiple colors,
the organized chaos
of Lisbon,
its feast of life,
its misery too.

It is morning.
You look at me.
We start to bond,
body and soul,
once more.

Suddenly,
my mind slips away.
From yesterday: a stair
in the maze of Alfama.
The curve of the hill
rounds me.

Desire fills me—
languor.

You enter me.
The city follows you
in your movement.
She fills me with her perfumes.

Her moist immodesty
pours out surges of her mystery.
I see her lovers from every street.

I feel the tide of her bodies.
In your arms, I become the city.

Love Alchemy

II PASSION

Yours, Spontaneously

Will I Dare You?

Sensing

The Red Snow

In This Silence

Yours, Spontaneously

By Sam Yau

I think of you
and out of the blue
I can feel you

Unconstrained
by the flow of time
it can be now
or backward
or forward

In any space
here
there
or anywhere
in the universe

It doesn't matter
which direction I move in
you always find me
fill my senses

It brings me joy
to detect any trace
of your presence
inside me
or outside

I am thrilled
to imagine how
you'd look at me
you'd hold me close
you'd take me
under your hands

Endless surprise

Endless delight

WILL I DARE *You?*

By Sophie Rouméas

I, a sometimes-hurt woman,
have dreamed a hundred times
the union of passion—
but a constructive one—
one that raises its frequency
and manifests pure energy.

Last night, you looked at me,
a sacred magnitude in your eyes.
Oh my god, is it me you see?

A rush of surprise.
I, explorer of the senses,
will I support his faith?

Your name means pure water.
I open my source to you.

I'm not alone anymore.
I found my earthquake—
the one who rides me—
the one who makes me want
to pause before daring
to step into his sun.

I arrive
on the surface of sacred restraint,
at the top of the mountain,
deep within my soul,
on the edge of your heart.

From your epicenter,
you look at me.

I'm coming to vibrate you,
will I dare you?

Will I Dare You?

We need a varied garden,
a nomadic and deep anchoring,
a desire
to love,
a generosity
to honor,
a heart that wishes for completeness—
but can be happy alone—
to support this intensity
within oneself.

I feel your thousand lives:
one who walks the path,
one who dares to reinvent it.
One who succeeds in everything,
one who is not attached to success.
One who acts in poetics,
one who loves as a scientist.
One who walks with his eyes to the sky
and who explores the depths of the break.

Sophie Rouméas

Molecular agitation,
moment of refraction,
you are allied to dispersion
and re-harmonization.

We become
our own new sequence:
a common destiny
on the random variable.

I can't resist playing
your effusive octaves.

You encourage my boldness,
will I dare all the way?

Sensing

By Sam Yau

The tenderness
of your velvet curves
glides against my body
I die for it to linger

Enraptured by your fiery gaze
my eyes become a camera that
captures your ever-changing face
lighted by Love, emanating
your soul's radiance

Your whispers and moans
from our morning rendezvous
still reverberate in my ears

The nectar of your passion
gusting out from every pore
of your sensuous body
ordains mine with pearly glints

As your waves break upon my shore
I ride your numinous rhythm to heaven

Your familiar scent still
permeates the space between us
I will savor its last trace
nor will I forget how you taste

This joy is ineffable

Sense me the way I sense you
you'll know how much I love you

THE RED *Snow*

By Sophie Rouméas

Soaring in the morning,
the wave of her desire
is growing.

Her lover, however,
although very close,
does not yet suspect
the inner rubedo
contained in her
sacral lair.

She comes and goes
like a serene sunrise.
But within, her spirit
is boiling.

The fire grows
exponentially.

The center
is consumed,
even her heart is
playing with her,
accelerating
in synchronicity.

She is waiting for the moment.
Like nature,
who loves the roundness
of the cyclical element.

She delights in these intense instances,
the sensuality
she doesn't immediately reveal
in her countenance,
not even in her sparkling eyes.

The moon above
continues her oracle.
From her temple,
she amplifies
the rising tides.

The lady slips into her red dress.
The offering cup fills up.
At nightfall, she will go,
offer a few drops of her essence
upon the immaculate white snow.

She takes her man's hand—
the wave is at its peak.
Come.

IN THIS *Silence*

By Sam Yau

I love to take a leave of absence
from my mental chatter
in the mindless rush of life

The tyranny of thoughts
comes to rest
and my senses expand

Now the world is ready
to reveal what was hidden
sights unseen
sounds unheard
bodily sensations unfelt

O my dear lover
I feel your body through
your palm
which my palm clasps
you are now my own flesh

In this silence
I enter your temple

I feel you now
your heartbeat
your breath
the rush of your arteries' blood
the warmth of your body
the familiarity of your energy

I enter a hall of remembrance
this one specific to
our rendezvous in Paris

You whisper in my ears
glide your body against mine
taste my lips divine

Images from this memory
finally catch up with me

I can no longer hold back
even though you are
on the other side of the globe

Love Garden

A New Garden

Your Inner Garden

Invitation to Your Senses

Love in a Cage

A NEW Garden

By Sophie Rouméas

I like to create with him,
to emanate our garden
of togetherness.

I revisit mine within—
unexplored plots,
flowers he may like,
ones I want to share.

He is there, smiling,
at the entrance of my garden.

I open my heart wider
and invite him in,
melting with happiness.

I let myself be visited—timidly,
then plainly.

In his energy,
the imprint of the loving gardener.
I like his character.

A New Garden

I step to the entrance
of his garden.
Inhale the multiple perfumes,
gently touch
the flowers of his soul.
Curious, I taste the spume of his dreams.

The foliage of his thoughts
leads me to the sap of his poetry.
The wind of humanity,
swirling and diverse, feeds
the prose of his philosophy.

Now, we are going to explore
this new universe
that we are composing together.

We combine our harmonies—
you garden my heart,
I sow yours.

Our entrances embrace,
we open our distances
and become One.

Our world is bursting with its spring.
A new season is beginning.
We patiently cultivate
the realm of our mission.

In between your lands and mine,
there are our traditions in fusion.
I enjoin the memories of my ancestors
to those you have collected from yours.

We shuffle Master Time's cards—
you mingle your essence with mine,
I embrace your eastern roots.

One by one, our differences become
bridges between your center and mine.
A new alchemy arises,
preceding inception of our creations.

In our cocreated garden, there is
your music and mine.
Both of us, conductors of our new notation.
Both of us, interpreters of our new happiness.

YOUR INNER Garden

By Sam Yau

There is an inner garden
a world only two can share

True love cannot be found
but it can be cultivated
in the magical realm of
love and intimacy

When you find homes in each other's hearts
your love sparkles like diamonds
your garden becomes a glorious Eden
your love heals your family and the world
you see beauty all around you

When you find homes in each other's bodies
your garden becomes sacred temple grounds
the passion's flame blazes like the sun
your soul is palpably felt like never before
you see sensuality all around you

Your garden blossoms
in a thousand fragrances of intimacy
that is the essence and purpose of love
the surest path to ecstasy

Your Inner Garden

Its seeds originate
from a deep soul connection
that cascades into
unimaginable intimacy
in all dimensions
of your being

Soul
mind
emotion
and body

The seeds' DNA comes from
the melding of both your essences

As you flourish and grow into
better versions of yourselves
so will your garden grow into
a more aromatic version of itself

Its soil is not tilled
from shallow promises
but a deep commitment
to one another

Sam Yau

Its water flows from hearts
of mellow tenderness
pure loving presence
deep sharing
and vulnerability
with one another

Intimacy and passion reinforce
each other in an endless circuitry

Love without intimacy fades
Intimacy without love feels hollow

You reap what you sow

Tend your garden well

The beauty of your inner garden
is made manifest
as the joy and bliss
of your union

INVITATION TO YOUR *Senses*

By Sophie Rouméas

The fragrance of my lover—
embedded in my memory.

An unspeakable presence,
this imprint on soul mystery.

My mind roams
then murmurs,
surrender to serendipity.

I surrender,
come what may.

A color—a carmine red
that throbs—activates.
I recognize the feeling
of Her infusing me.

But who is She?
She who invites herself
into any room of consciousness?

She is
the vibration in his voice
as he speaks his sentiments,
reverberating
through the wooden bench
as a harp song in my cells.

Invitation to Your Senses

She's the fire in his eyes
when he greets me with desire,
She is that pearl drop of water
in the morning, after a rain,
that sparkles with filaments
on the leaves of a white rose.

She is the grace of reason
when words dance together.
She crowns—with her passion
the one who tames her—with patience.

She was said to be cursed,
deemed unfit for wisdom.
She is banished from such houses
and praised in such temples.

Pure under prisms,
a friend to painters and poets,
she is everywhere, an artist
birthing her canvas for eternity.

She can be learned,
even unlearned,
depending on whether you want
to reinvent yourself.

Sophie Rouméas

Don't get me wrong,
She will always be rebellious.
Breathe her in, she inspires you.
Forget her, she fades away.

The usefulness you find in her
depends only on your presence
to let your senses be opened
to let her transcend you at all.

She is the whisper of your dreams
unveiling the audacious you.
She is the seed of your ideas
to manifest your vocation.

An indomitable spirit
of life, matter and emotions,
she arises from a naturalness.
She is She, He, and Plural.
She conjugates all the time.

Be observant, be patient,
invite your guest:
Sensuality is at your door.

Love in a Cage

By Sophie Rouméas

I wish a freed love with you,
a love that flies like a dragonfly,
lights like a Good Luck lantern,
pollinates like a hummingbird,
reverberates like a drum.

I wish a succulent love with you,
a love that tastes like a piece of heaven
and smells like the finest rose
in the finest garden.

I wish us to be a new specie
who dares to date
despite religion, philosophy,
conventions—
any differences.

You and I are not staying in the cage,
we are journeying together.

The sky becomes our room; clouds, our bed;
stars, our candles; the moon, our piece of art;
and the sun, our alchemist,

joins with our new waters
to grow new flowers on earth.

Love and Growth

Interdependence

Hold the Space

Reciprocity

Letter to My Sons

Love and Religion

Interdependence

By Sam Yau

Lover, do not lose yourself
for I cherish who you are
and the way you live your life

Don't please me
love me

In pleasing me
you lose part of you

In loving
you become expansive

Do not change
any part of yourself
because you want to fit in

Allow yourself
to change
in a natural and
intentional way
as we melt our lives
into each other

Like two circles
coming together
not all parts of us
will overlap

We will learn
what parts will remain
separate but together
with full support
from one another

Our life is
a dance between
independence and
interdependence

Each of us
self-sufficient
we are fuller and happier
when we join our lives together
in all our uniqueness

Our differences
will bring richness
to our shared life

We will remain curious and explore
the vastness of the universe that is us

Let us promise to share ourselves deeply
always believing in the best of each other

In mirroring each other
we find the best in us
we are still unaware of

We will dance this dance well

We will grow well together

HOLD THE Space

By Sophie Rouméas

Don't be upset with me, my love.
With you, I grow.

I'm no longer at the core of my strength,
nor am I dressed in certitude.
With you, I express.

I explore the roots of our future
while staying present in our present.
With you, I dare.

I wish to bring you my colors,
my own light and completeness.
With you, I trust.

As a newcomer in the forest
of your life,
I walk the path with an open heart.
With you, I learn.

I am conscious of your people
and your family of trees.
It is an honor to land on your land.
With you, I care.

It's no small thing to leave a nest,
a known network of roots,
and dare to fly high and far away.
With you, I choose.

But my love, not everyday
do I reveal brightest colors,
nor do I feel grounded while suspended
nor do I feel safe while in between.

In your forest, there is a balance.
Homeostasis prefers the known
to the unknown; to a new species
daring to plant a new seed
in the soil of the sacred ground.

Darling, can I express my doubts
and not have them dissipate in the wind,
only to return as a panoply of clouds?

But if the rain helps the seed to root,
then it will bring its fruits to the birds
and the birds will sing
the taste of the New.

Still, the rain must be light
to respect the alchemy
of the numinous space
as a nurturing element.
With you, I love.

Reciprocity

By Sam Yau

Before I meet you
I seek to love myself
unconditionally

After I fall in love with you
I will seek to love you
unconditionally

Will you do the same for me

Before I meet you
I love who I am

After I fall in love with you
I will love you for who you are

Will you do the same for me

Before I meet you
I have my way of life and my boundaries

After I fall in love with you
I will respect your way of life and your boundaries

Will you do the same for me

Before I meet you
I am on my journey for growth

After I fall in love with you
I will support your journey for growth

Will you do the same for me

I will strive to be free
from the fear of losing you
from jealousy
from control
from codependency

Will you do the same for me

If we do our best
we will grow individually and together
we will love in clear light without shadow
we will balance love for self and partner

The secret to unconditional love

Reciprocity

Letter to My Sons

By Sophie Rouméas

The day I became a mom,
I was already far from the world of my childhood.
Though still young, I learned to navigate
between the troubled waters of the past
and hope for a happy future.

For you, son of my early maturity,
I cultivated the audacity to be a mother
while others were working on their careers.

In your father, I found
my rooting as young woman in flower,
he became my reason to love
in a saving and passionate way.

I loved carrying the dawn of futurity within me,
to make the most beautiful gift for your father,
and for you, the sweetest welcome.
From the elders, I was given
the right to choose my freedom.
I decided there was no age
more appropriate than an inspired love.

You grew up
with beautiful light in your heart.
Your orphan father rocked you happily
when you were a baby.

When our lives became
more chaotic than serene,
I had to tap into the elders'
strength to leave.

I had to become a confident young mother.
You shaped yourself in that time of the two of us,
created your own garden
without your father.
At nightfall, I would ask the elders to pray
with me to keep you safe.

Then, one renewed, youthful evening,
a man walked towards me,
time suspended in the air.
I kissed him whole and fully.

Letter to My Sons

Welcome, my son of the second flowering.
We have united our destinies with your father,
who embraced me with your brother
like his natural family.

We plunged first into the lagoon waters,
wove the joy of friendships,
confronted some dragons together,
then joined our two fluids to birth you.

Our family thus grew.
Your father, your brother and I—
we loved you straightaway.

From our little buddha you became
the amazing young man you are today.

Between being an active woman,
a home and work partner with your father,
an attentive mother, with all
my dimensions—my rights and my duties,
caring for our family,
I could do and be everything from morning to night.

Sophie Rouméas

Then, one day, the inevitable.
From queen and king of our realm,
we became no longer inseparable.
A period of torment—
our values, our dreams collided.
The for-life puzzle came apart,
a divorce was granted.

Family law came to the fore,
we separated our property and set rules
that a judge endorsed on a piece of paper.

You became one of the 1.6 million French children
who live in blended families.
To be conscious parents for you,
we will always have to overcome our discord.

I had to tap into my strength again,
to be a single mother again,
to recreate serenity.

From those years in halftones,
I took the right to train myself
to better understand human nature,
to heal me and then to heal others.

Letter to My Sons

I made peace with my duties
so, for you both love remains your right,
and the center of our destinies.

We, your family, will always care for you.

My sons, you are on your way.
May life dance with you,
may you love and feel loved,
may the trajectory of your soul
be toward light, happiness and fulfillment.

The recurrent involution of our humanity
could never extinguish
your freshness and dignity.

Our world is changing.
You are part of the change.
Whatever your choices,
I wish for you consciousness and confidence.

Feminism is reconciling with the masculine,
men and women are redefining themselves.
Don't be afraid of the woman; learn her.
And let her learn you.

Sophie Rouméas

Some will always believe
that woman was created from Adam's rib,
and the rights of women
are extracted from (hu)Man rights.

But I know you know:
Woman and man are each composed of
80% water, cells full of vacuum,
star particles,
a brain, a heart and a soul,
many miracles, the first being Love
(whatever excesses have been associated with it).

Every human being has the right to love and be loved,
and the responsibility to respect life inside and around.
If one makes happiness his or her quest—
even if one pursues no quest—
let it be known that all paths begin within.

With all my love,
Mum

Love and Religion

By Sophie Rouméas

The loving nature
of a romantic relationship
has the power to elevate
the human spirit
toward the divine.

Within a soul, seeded with
particles of every possibility,
the pure matter of love
assembles and intensifies
until the birth of unity.

My love,
I welcome your religion
with no doubt or concern,
because I know we both answer
to the same divine laws:
love, respect, and creation.

By Sophie Rouméas

I met you at Omega,
the ultimate place for personal growth.
It feels now like it was a homecoming,
like a gateway we walked through
to enter the port of our hearts.

There was a moment
when our souls connected.
You were aware of our possible magic,
I was starting a journey.

Sigma, Alpha, in the separate
toboggans of our lives,
we continued as parallel universes,
each traveling our personal Euclidean alphabet
until nothing more important
could happen than
for us to meet completely.

Naked in the divine
of our souls,
we anchor at last—
not only in our intertwining brain waves
or the rearrangements of our destinies—
but in the union of our bodies.

Our Omega point is that purple heart—
the higher consciousness
is up to us to nourish and let flourish.

Our journey is a delight.
From Alpha to Omega,
I love our light.

Love and Healing

Return to Love

Return to Wholeness

Residual Matter

The Misunderstanding

Womanity's Shadow

Acceptance

RETURN TO

By Sam Yau

Love to our soul
is like air to our body

To heal is
to love again

RETURN TO Wholeness

By Sam Yau

Because of pain caused by trauma
you dissociate from your body

Because of hurt from wounding events
you disown them and their memories

Because of never receiving enough love
you feel you're not good enough

Because of fear of disapproval
you hide parts of you in shadow

You have lost so much of you

Brokenness
unspoken grief
emptiness

Gather all the parts you have discarded
include and transcend them
for you don't have to live there anymore

Soon you will discover
your true nature
you are precious
totally lovable
perfect

Come home to your body

Embrace the totality of your life's journey

Reclaim who you are

Discover the fullness
of being both divine and human

To heal
is to return to wholeness

RESIDUAL *Matter*

By Sophie Rouméas

I left this morning on
the day train of my thoughts—
my dreams of creativity,

your mood was not all sunshine,
there were clouds in your sky
that you would have liked to
point out to me.

Oblivious to your weather,
absorbed by the sky outside,
I walked out the door.

I carry you very high
in my heart
even when leaving the port
of our intimacy.

You were waiting for me to see
the shadowy distance
separating you
from yourself.

Evening finds us—
me closer to my dreams,
you, further from yours.

A smile on the edge of my lips,
I approach you for a kiss.

You look at me, a little bitter.
I have so many joys to announce to you,
I'm outside of the reach of your sadness,
you feel outside of my reality.

Sometimes, this residual matter
we are not aware of
is created from emotions and thoughts.

Today I am in joy, and you are in pain.

When we are unaligned for a time,
the one who feels lighter
has a choice:
an invitation to raise awareness,
her or his gaze turned toward the other.

The sharing of joy can wait,
difficulty cannot.

Now, I am facing the mirror as night falls.
My mind calms.
I refocus on the center of us.
I see your face again,
your drawn features,
I'm reviewing your morning energy.
Finally, I turn to you.

I walk toward our bed, our boat.
I enter our port, well-moored.
You left this morning in full swell,
and tonight, you have yet to return.

I take your hand in silence,
I listen to your heart's hurt rhythm.
I synchronize with your vibration
and welcome your frustration.

Sophie Rouméas

My love, I'm sorry.
If you want to talk to me,
I'm listening now.
You turn to me.

Finally, there she is.

I open the window to our universe,
we enter the starry sky together.
This evening,
we are transforming
copper dust into gold
again.

THE *Misunderstanding*

By Sam Yau

There are many days of happiness
sailing on the calm waters
of our meandering river

We discover our affinities and similarities
we look at each other
see our resemblance
our affection grows
through our familiarity

Hidden in the background is
a lifetime of different experiences

We come to the first rushing rapid
the wide chasm
between our cultures
our life experiences
good and bad times
in our past relationships

How they have crafted
a tinted lens we perceive each other through

Your innocent casual comment
sounds like judgment to me
I am hit by the hammer of your words

I lash out at
lightning speed with
an uncalled-for reaction sprung
from my past relationship trauma
that my self-awareness fails to catch

An outsized response to a non-existent
provocation, perceived incorrectly

The surprise hurt keeps us tongue-tied

Unwilling to disrupt days of good weather
we stay silent, aware
we are storing unresolved resentment
like gathering dark clouds

Thunder and lightning will strike again

My dear, I am sorry
I own it

I am dreaming of smooth waters
on a sunny cloudless day

Can we talk about it?

Womanity's Shadow

By Sophie Rouméas

Three ways can prevent me from appreciating you—
being out of tune with my femininity,
being a prisoner of my past and family story,
not perceiving the purity of your love.

I'd like to find the antidote
to these three possible shadows in the world.
I commit to looking into my own personal ones
without make-up, without trembling.

I was born a full woman,
connected to the moon and its tidal phases.
From my cycles, emotions are born.
When I dare to be mind, body, and spirit,
I am not afraid of my
hurly-burly fluctuations.

I become a temple
to welcome the flowers of your passion.

I carry past sorrows and joys,
those of my lineage of women and men.
From them,
I also received the gift of transmutation.
Life grants wisdom and clarity.
I am offered the choice to activate my comprehension
and get away from
the helter-skelter incarnations.

Embracing my ancestors
becomes the answer.

I am then free and whole in our becoming.
You, the man I've chosen—
whom I feel chosen by.

I receive and love you in acceptance
that your humanity is the same as mine—
you are also the fruit of two opposite stars.

Equidistant from earth to the divine,
I am moving my center of gravity
towards you.

Love, still, is the answer.

Acceptance

By Sam Yau

My curriculum was designed
for my growth in this lifetime

May I embrace all experiences
as they unfold on my path

May I know I am here
to live my unique life

May I refrain from
judging events as good or bad

May I be wise enough
not to compare my realities
with those of others

May I step into my healing
by accepting what is

May I forgive myself and others
and learn my lessons and move on

May I fully taste
each unfolding
and leave no trace
of guilt or shame
and feel joy again

Burdened by neither
the past nor the future
I live in the present moment
starting afresh each new day

Love AND ART

An Incessant Dialogue

Vincent

AN INCESSANT

By Sophie Rouméas

I

She has piercing eyes,
deep blue and translucent.
I freeze for a moment.
She is painted upon a canvas,
a woman created and initiated
by the hand of her painter.

I was in the streets of Saint Paul de Vence,
I felt drawn into the feast of the senses,
its thousand and one inspirations,
its awakened spirit,
its mad rushing portal.

I walk into a gallery.
The artist who owns it
starts giving a speech,
he has been waiting for someone
to deliver his philosophy.

He never stops philosophizing,
It's in his paintings,
He breathes it.

The painting is of his wife,
she is also a painter,
and both his muse and his partner.

II

Artists are chameleons.
they blend in their subjectivity and
bewitch yours,
invoke thought,
divert it, decomplexify it,
sometimes transform it, often
transcend it.

Art is an
invitation
arising every day
at the bend of the street.

It can be born of human intention
or a natural emergence:
the curve of a tree trunk,
interspersed with ivy in the evening sun,
a cloud's destiny in the divine light
the flight of a butterfly among the wheatgrass.

Art is a
conversation.
It opens us up to other countries,
to other melodies, to others than me.

It informs me of wars, torments,
concerns of the world,
of the heart and its destinations.

III

Art is Chagall, Da Vinci, De Sainte Phalle,
it's Schubert, Beethoven, the village pianist—
all found in the streets of Saint Paul de Vence.

It is Picasso's *Dove of Peace*,
Schnabel's purple *Waterfall*.

Passage witness, message bearer,
art is the world that expresses itself,
even values and positions.

It's the perfume of a woman, her blue wake in the street,
it is an exquisite chocolate dome from a great starred chef,

it's the round of the senses,
yours, mine and what we make of them.

Vincent

By Sam Yau

You were born on
the first anniversary of
the death of your mother's firstborn

You were cast in the identical name
in memory of your brother

Every year on your birthday
your mother took you
to the cemetery
where he was buried

You were a phantom of
your brother for whom
your mom never ceased grieving

You were never celebrated
or loved for who you are

The world was cold and unsafe for you
unloved and unappreciated for your gift
you received only contempt and scorn

Yet, in the deep recesses of your soul
you immerse yourself in a rich inner life
unbeknownst to the world

You see what no one else can see
you have no choice but to paint it

You show your love for the world
it is never returned while you're alive

In nature you find
the beauty that nourishes you
the wellspring that unfolds your genius
the transcendence that knows
the wondrous power of brilliant color

that reverberates in
the souls of millions
who see what you saw
the blue night sky with
bright swirling yellow stars
one summer night in Saint Rémy

Love AND CONSCIOUSNESS

Traveling in Reality

The Path

Conscious Silence

Step into the Stream

Archetypes

The Nature of Love

TRAVELING IN *Reality*

By Sophie Rouméas

The chill rain of an autumn day
frames the splendor of the Tuileries;
the opulence of the Opera Garnier.
Among endless beguiling windows
of art, elegance, promise and grace,
infused with the faith of Notre-Dame
and the passion of a gospel concert
in the American Cathedral rue George V,
I am filled with Paris.

At the bend of Rivoli,
a man on his knees, shirtless.
Without even one arm.
I try to guess his age.
He looks too young to
have survived World War II.
I wonder if he was
from Eastern Europe.
Maybe he was part of a gang.
What could leave a human
without arms?

I cry from the inside.
I walk by him slowly.
There is a man
helping him drink
some water.

How can he drink
when there is no one
to assist him?

I do not close my eyes
I do not
close my eyes. I do
not close my eyes.

I am late for my train,
but I cannot walk away.

How many times in my life
have I not taken the time
to see the hard reality?

I breathe a gentle smile,
grab all the euros
I have on me—
maybe enough for a few meals?

I meet his eyes.
I feel his dignity.
Can I participate in your day?

I want to
connect with him at the right level,
not make him feel less-than,
honor him.

Two bright,
bottomless eyes say
yes.

He returns to his water.

The caregiver is too busy to
catch my gaze—
an angel consumed with his task.

This moment won't leave me
even on the train home,
even miles away.

I beg myself to stay
in the emotions of my heart,
to continue to walk the days
of this world of contrasts.

This morning,
I prayed the Providence.

May each moment
bring him closer
to a softer day,
to leave this October soil,
and to reprogram his trajectory
to the beauty of life.

Will you pray with me?

THE *Path*

By Sam Yau

Beauty is the sun that
illuminates my inner journey
it stills my heart with peace
it rests my mind with joy

Beauty is the breeze that refreshes me
it softens me when my truth feels harsh
it revives me when my goodness feels draining

My sense of beauty knows my name alone

Truth is what I've learned from my life
your truth remains a hypothesis to me
it is not mine until I experience it

All I can commit to live by is my personal truth

All my goodness springs from my heart
my conscience is my only judge
your heart doesn't know mine

Do not judge me as good or bad
you know neither my situation
nor the context shaped by my life story

The measure of my goodness is mine alone

Isn't love the highest value of how I live

Love is the wellspring of these three virtues

If I choose love as my guide
then I can know with certainty

I am on the right path to live
my beauty
my truth and
my goodness

CONSCIOUS *Silence*

By Sophie Rouméas

Souls are imprisoned by
incessant noisiness.
Silence sets us free
and reignites our senses.

There was a time when
silence annoyed me.
From the silence of an empty house
to that of people around me,
I felt this childish loneliness,
like a soul sadly circumscribed.

Hence, my quest for incessant dialogue,
from which I cultivated
my passion for understanding—
now, silence, the good one,
never ceases to remind me of
its usefulness to my reinitiated senses.

At a certain point, time
is no longer just a time,
it is how my awakened perception
receives the sweet song
of a soul that marvels.

Alpha, theta, my waves
are enriched by this silent,
holy-grail transcendence.

I can make silence
my friend; guidance
for my mind entranced.

Silence offers me its virtues.
A deep presence
to what is.

Silence teaches me.
The next action, a better reaction.
From silence I can arise,
align with nature's wisdom.

Silence connects me.
I join with the reality of our universe,
from its tiniest grain
to our complete Oneness.

Silence dissolves me.
Then, I am aware of you.
You, my love, my children,
my neighbors, my fellow humans,
you, that I have never known.

Silence serves me.
And just as much, I serve it.
It is a dance,
a reconciliation with time.

For the grace of peace,
I return to the present—
the key
that activates
conscious silence.

STEP INTO THE

By Sam Yau

You seek to control
the trajectory of your path

What if you're a mere witness
in the divine flow of your life

You strive to win
the race against fate

What if random events are arranged
by the hands of destiny in disguise

You burn the candle at both ends
straining to make your dreams come true

What if your seemingly solid reality
is only a dream of your soul
to experience the human journey

In silence
you will know you are part
of the cosmic consciousness

Step into the stream
swim with the current

You will come to know
the purpose of your soul

In the interplay of destiny and free will
your actions will be spontaneously guided

Archetypes

By Sophie Rouméas

How does one recognize those who are awakened?
Is it by their ability to define
who they are in their soul
and live aligned with?
How they navigate the ocean of interconnectedness?

Plato, Jung, Spinoza, and countless others
mapped the human psyche with archetypes.

We wish to be free, defined by our aspirations,
not only by our actions and reactions.

To succeed in life
is to grasp the usefulness of these codifications,
learn from our behaviors and their implications—
then break free.

When I meet the Other,
I am not in front of a Rebel, a Priestess, a Judge or a Lover,
I am in front of you, with the same rights, the first of which
is to be free and equal in dignity.

Whoever you are, you were not created in my image—
I am not a reflection of you.
We are face to face
to discover the richness of human evolution.

I can ignore what I don't understand about you,
reject what I don't recognize—
or appreciate where you are,
meet you in the middle,
neither at your house nor at mine,
in a space of respect and curiosity,
creating room for sharing and learning
in conversation.

One by one,
I mindfully deactivate the codes of my past.
Then, my shadows can't activate yours,
nor yours activate mine.

Transference disappears from our reality.
I, you, we
bathe in the lit flow of unity.

From fractional archetypes,
we become the fractal
of harmony.

THE NATURE OF Love

By Sam Yau

Love binds
causes things
to come together
to interact
to co-create
to evolve
in an endless cycle of love

Love is the subtle vibration
that underlies the ocean of
interpenetrating fields
of energy and matter

Love is more fundamental than
electromagnetic, nuclear
and gravitational forces

Love invokes matter to become
life through alchemy

It is the mother of all feelings
it is the origin of all unions

Of life, love is
the sweetest nectar
the balm that heals
life's wounds, and
its deepest longing

Its shadow is fear
fear of loss of love
fear of loneliness

The birth of all births
the creator of all creations
the thrust of all creative impulses

It is disguised as thousands of things
amid which we have forgotten our true essence

Love subdivides itself
into many forms of beauty

Beauty is in the eyes of the lover
the one who can no longer love
cannot see beauty in anything

Even truth is like a ray of light
that can be bent
in opposite directions
by the perspectives
of love
or fear

If you are a lover of all things
your stream of joy and bliss
is unceasing

You then live as your true being

You are love itself

ABOUT THE POETS

Sam Yau

Sam has re-invented his life several times, from a six-month-old baby on a refugee boat, to a penniless student from a distant land, to the CEO of a billion-dollar corporation, to the chairman of an iconic pioneering center for personal growth, to a poet who writes about the soul's journey, life's vicissitudes, trauma and healing, consciousness, and mysticism.

Sam has an MBA in finance from the University of Chicago. He lives with his sixteen-year-old daughter in Laguna Beach. Sam enjoys music, hiking, and active travel.

Sam can be reached at sam@samyaupoetry.com.

Sophie Rouméas

For some people, music is their words; for others, words are their music. Passionate about words and their ability to trigger emotions, memories and thoughts, Sophie infuses them in her therapeutic work as she leads meditation, hypnosis sessions, and family constellations.

In 2021 she compiled and published her first anthology, *J'ai vécu la même chose que toi*, written with twelve co-authors. The best-seller testifies to the resilience displayed by these young women who recovered from breast cancer as a message of hope and encouragement for the families affected by this ordeal.

Born in the French Alps, nature has always been a source of creativity for Sophie; encouraging intuition, listening and expression in others, she created the motto *Let's voice your soul!* and embodies it through her professional and artistic projects.

The meeting of the two poets occurred in New York, during a workshop on past lives followed by a concert dedicated to the poet Rumi; after years of artistic friendship, their mutual encouragement to develop their poetic writing naturally manifested into *Souls in Love*.

ARTWORK CREDITS

SOULS IN LOVE

Souls in Love – by Sam Yau
Painting by Gustav Klimt, *Fulfilment*, 1905

The Hummingbird – by Sophie Rouméas
Painting by Martin Johnson Heade, *Orchid and Hummingbird near a Mountain Waterfall*, 1902

I Can't Wait to Meet You – by Sam Yau
Painting by Olena Zavakevych, inspired by the poem *I Can't Wait to Meet You*, 2020

Souls' Encounter – by Sophie Rouméas
Painting by Wen Zhengming, *Huishan Tea Party*, 1518

KINDRED SPIRITS

Infused – by Sam Yau
Photography by Donyanedomam

Wine Tasting – by Sam Yau
Photography by RomoloTavani

How Do We Know – by Sophie Rouméas
Painting by Marc Chagall, *Lovers with Half Moon*, 1926

Love and Shadow – by Sam Yau
Painting by Pierre Auguste Cot, *The Storm*, 1880

LOVE ALCHEMY

I Transcendence

Transcendence – by Sophie Rouméas
Photography by Torsakarin

Re-creating – by Sam Yau
Photography by -M-I-S-H-A-

The Gem-Seed of Intention – by Sophie Rouméas
Photography by Robert Doisneau, *Le Baiser de l'Hôtel de Ville*, 1950

Full Union in Love – by Sam Yau
Photography by drferry

Lisbon – by Sophie Rouméas
Photography by Olga Gavrilova

II Passion

Yours, Spontaneously – by Sam Yau
Painting by Marc Chagall, *Birthday*, 1887

Will I Dare You? – by Sophie Rouméas
Photography by Vera Petruk

Sensing – by Sam Yau
Painting by Pierre Auguste Cot, *Spring*, 1873

The Red Snow – by Sophie Rouméas
Photography by Kharchenko Irina 7

In This Silence – by Sam Yau
Painting by Frederic Lord Leighton, *Flaming June*, 1895

LOVE GARDEN

A New Garden – by Sophie Rouméas
Painting by Sandro Botticelli, *The Birth of Venus*, 1485

Your Inner Garden – by Sam Yau
Photography by WeStudio

Invitation to Your Senses – by Sophie Rouméas
Painting by Giorgio Dante, *Poi Tornò All' Eterna Fonte*, 2021

Love in a Cage – by Sophie Rouméas
Photography by Alex Liew

LOVE AND GROWTH

Interdependence – by Sam Yau
Photography by avid_creative

Hold the Space – by Sophie Rouméas
Photography by Deep Green

Reciprocity – by Sam Yau
Photography by inarik

Letter to My Sons – by Sophie Rouméas
Painting by William Adolphe Bouguereau, Rest, 1879

Love and Religion – by Sophie Rouméas
Photography by Noon Virachada

💜 – by Sophie Rouméas
Painting by Vincent Van Gogh, Irises, 1889

LOVE AND HEALING

Return to Love – by Sam Yau
Sculpture by Antonio Canova, *Psyche Revived by Cupid's Kiss*, 1793

Return to Wholeness – by Sam Yau
Photography by Bernsten

Residual Matter – by Sophie Rouméas
Photography by Serts

The Misunderstanding – by Sam Yau
Photography by Givaga

Womanity's Shadow – by Sophie Rouméas
Artwork by Saint Michael's School of Divinity, *The Divine Feminine*

Acceptance – by Sam Yau
Photography by Don White

LOVE AND ART

An Incessant Dialogue – by Sophie Rouméas
Painting by Konstentin Makowsky, *The Muse of Poesie*, 1886

Vincent – by Sam Yau
Painting by Vincent van Gogh, *The Starry Night*, 1889

LOVE AND CONSCIOUSNESS

Traveling in Reality – by Sophie Rouméas
Photography by Den Kuvalem

The Path – by Sam Yau
Photography by jimfeng

Conscious Silence – by Sophie Rouméas
Photography by Iropa

Step into the Stream – by Sam Yau
Photography by Joecho-16

Archetypes – by Sophie Rouméas
Photography by Nikada

The Nature of Love – by Sam Yau
Photography by sun ok

www.ingramcontent.com/pod-product-compliance
Lightning Source LLC
Chambersburg PA
CBHW050738110526
44590CB00002B/21